Understanding Personal Finance Skills

MONEY, GOALS AND BUDGETING

ROBYN HARDYMAN

PowerKiDS press.
New York

Published in 2018 by **The Rosen Publishing Group, Inc.**
29 East 21st Street, New York, NY 10010

Cataloging-in-Publication Data

Names: Hardyman, Robyn.
Title: Understanding money goals and budgeting / Robyn Hardyman.
Description: New York : PowerKids Press, 2018. | Series: Money skills for kids | Includes index.
Identifiers: ISBN 9781508153764 (pbk.) | ISBN 9781499434927 (library bound) | ISBN 9781499434828 (6 pack)
Subjects: LCSH: Finance, Personal--Juvenile literature. | Budgets, Personal--Juvenile literature.| Financial literacy--
    Juvenile literature.| Finance--Juvenile literature.
Classification: LCC HG179.H349 2018 | DDC 332.024--dc23

Produced for Rosen by Calcium
Editors for Calcium: Sarah Eason and Jennifer Sanderson
Designers for Calcium: Paul Myerscough and Jennie Child
Picture researcher: Jennifer Sanderson

Photo Credits: Cover: Shutterstock: wong sze yuen. Inside: Shutterstock: Absolute India 1, 18, Alan Bailey 13, David
Litman 11, Dean Bertoncelj 15, Blend Images 20, Fizkes 17, Gorillaimages 9, JNP 7, Jordi C 25, Mangostock 23,
Monkey Business Images 4, 8, 26, 31, Nestor Rizhniak 27, Poznyakov 7, Sergey Novikov 29, Sylvie Bouchard 14,
Wavebreakmedia 21.

Manufactured in the United States of America
CPSIA Compliance Information: Batch BS17PK: For Further Information contact Rosen Publishing, New York, New York at 1-800-237-9932.

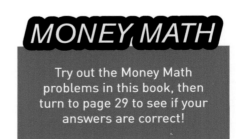

MONEY MATH

Try out the Money Math
problems in this book, then
turn to page 29 to see if your
answers are correct!

CONTENTS

MANAGE YOUR MONEY

We all need money for the **basic** things we need—our homes, the clothes we wear, the food we eat. Life is full of **expenses**. Whether we have an allowance or earn money from working, each of us needs to manage our cash. You can learn money managing skills now and gain control of your future.

To pay for the things we want, such as bikes and vacations, we need to learn how to manage our money.

STAYING IN CONTROL OF YOUR MONEY

The best way to stay in control of our money is to know how much we have and how much we are going to spend. If we know that, we can make a plan. We can figure out if we have enough money to pay for the things we cannot do without, like food. Hopefully, we have enough to cover the basics. Then we can figure out what to do with the rest of our money.

Imagine it's your birthday and your relatives give you $30. It's hard not to rush out and spend it all at once. The stores are always full of things to tempt us, and it feels great to know you can go shopping for something fun. The smart thing to do, though, is to think ahead. Maybe that is the last money you will have coming in for several months. If you spend it all now, you will have nothing to spend in the future. When a new video game is released or your friends suggest a trip to the movies, you won't be able to **afford** it.

HOW TO GET THERE

The answer is to think carefully about what you want to spend your money on, now and in the future. This is all about setting goals. Once you have your money goals, you can figure out how to achieve them and make your money work for you. To do this, you need to make up a **budget**. A budget is a plan of your spending and **saving**. Figuring out a budget helps prevent money problems. It also makes it easier and more fun to spend money when we know we can afford it.

SHOW ME THE MONEY

In the United States, the Bureau of Engraving and Printing makes about 38 million bills of different values every day, with a total value of about $540 million. Almost all of them are used to replace old bills that have worn out.

THINK ABOUT GOALS

When you have decided that you are going to take control of your **finances**, it means that you must watch the money you earn, spend, and save. To set your money goals, first you need to think about the money you spend on the basics. Then you can plan for the rest.

SPEND IT

When we are young, we do not have to think too much about the essential costs of everyday living. The adults around us usually take care of the basics, such as rent, food, heat, and electricity. You may have some things you need to spend your money on, though. If you are given an allowance, your parents may expect you to pay for certain things with it. Maybe you need to buy birthday gifts for your friends and family. If so, you need to plan ahead for those expenses. Maybe you need to pay for your lunch at school each day. It is up to you to make sure that you have enough for these things. If you spend your entire allowance on other things, you will be stuck.

When you are older, your finances become a little more complex. You may have more opportunities to earn money. You certainly have more things to spend it on, too! You'll want to spend money going out with friends and on clothes, music, books, and many other things. When you go to college or get a job and your own home, you must learn about living independently. That is a big responsibility, and it takes planning. You really have to know your goals. If you develop good money habits when you are younger, you will find it much easier to be responsible as an adult.

GOOD SPENDERS

Spending money is easy! We are surrounded by stores full of things, and there are commercials that try to get us to part with our cash. Since we do not have unlimited money, we need to be good spenders. This means being smart. It means knowing what things cost and figuring out how we will pay for them.

SAVE IT

There are always things we must spend our money on, but we also need to save some for later. Saving is a really important part of thinking about your money goals. Saving money can be difficult, especially if you do not have much to start with, but **every little bit counts**. It is easier if you think about what you are saving up for. Keep your eye on the prize! With every dollar you save, you're moving closer to your **goal**.

Really wanting something can be all the motivation you need to save up for it. When it is finally yours, you'll feel great!

MONEY MATH

You want to buy a skateboard that costs $30. You earn $8 a week for doing chores. Your basic expenses cost $3.00 a week. How many weeks would you have to save up before you could buy your new board?

SEE PAGE 29 FOR THE ANSWER!

KEEP TRACK

If you are going to be in charge of your money, it helps to keep a good record. If you know exactly what you are spending, you can build up a picture of where your money is going. Then you can plan ahead for the things you need and maybe stop spending on some of the things you do not really need.

KEEP A SPENDING JOURNAL

It's time to keep track of your spending. The easiest way to do this is to keep a journal. In a lined notebook, write out the dates for one month, with one date on each line. Then make five columns across the page. Here, you can record the amounts of money you spend each day. If you make many purchases every day, you may need more than five columns. Each column is a category of things you typically buy, such as "Basic Needs" or "Comic Books." You could label the fourth column "Other" for expenses that do not fit into any of your categories. The final column should be titled "Day Total." This is for the total you spend each day.

Each day, write down what you spend in the correct column. Some days you may spend nothing, but other days will be more expensive. This is common when it comes to spending. At the end of each day, add up your total, and write it in the last column. At the end of the month, add up all the figures in each column. The column total will show you how much you have spent in each category.

Just a few minutes each day spent recording your spending will soon show you where your cash is going.

AT A GLANCE

When you add up all the figures in the last column, you will get a grand total of what you have spent during the month. How did it go? Were you surprised at how much you spent on games or snacks? Did you have a bigger purchase that you were not expecting? Using a journal is a great way to see at a glance where your money is going. It will help you set your goals for the future.

Washing cars is a service that other people may be willing to pay you for. It is a good way to earn extra cash.

SERVICES

We do not spend our money only on goods or things. Much of our money is spent on services, which are the things that other people provide for us. Services include things like heat and electricity for our homes or help in the house or backyard. Babysitters provide a service, too. Teenagers can earn money babysitting for neighbors.

WHAT IS COMING IN?

You have completed your spending journal, so now you have a good idea of where your money is going each week or month. It is time to find out how much money you have coming in and where it is coming from!

INCOME

Money that comes in to us is called **income**. We can earn it by working, or we receive it as an allowance or gift. Or we may find it outside on the street! Wherever it comes from, it is ours to spend or save. If we are going to set out goals and make a plan for our finances, we need to know how much we have.

DEPENDING ON MONEY

It is also important to know if the money is going to keep coming in. Some kinds of income are more reliable than others. You may receive an allowance every week. You can depend on it coming in, and your plans can be based on getting it regularly. Bigger gifts are less reliable. Holidays and birthdays come much less often. You probably do not know if or how much you are going to receive, either. Last year, your aunt may have given you $30, but this year, she may give you clothes or another gift instead — or even no gift at all! This means that we cannot depend on those amounts coming in.

It is just the same for adults. They may have a regular income from their work that they can depend on, as long as their job lasts. Once a year, some people receive a bonus, an extra payment from their **employer**, if they or their business has done really well. They may also find extra work at certain times of year. For example, if a job involves working outdoors, employees might work and earn more money in the summer when the weather is better than in the winter.

People who work seasonal jobs, such as harvesting vegetables, may work other jobs in the winter.

MONEY MATH

Your allowance is $20 a month. For your last birthday, you were given $40, and on New Year's Eve, you were given $30. How much did you receive altogether in the last year (12 months)?

SEE PAGE 29 FOR THE ANSWER!

SET YOUR GOALS

Now you are on your way to controlling your money. You know how much is coming in and how you are spending it. With all this information, you can set your goals and create a plan.

MAKE YOUR MONEY WORK

What do you want your money to do for you? Money is no use to us as bills and coins—there is no point just collecting it to look at. We can't eat money, it doesn't keep us warm, and it isn't much fun to play with. Money is used to pay for things, so the first thing is to decide what you want it to pay for. We all know we can buy something only if we have enough money to pay for it. Have you ever found yourself in this situation when out shopping? You thought you had enough for a snack, but at the checkout, you find that you still need 10 cents. The only thing you can do is put the snack back on the shelf and leave the store, feeling disappointed.

FUTURE GOALS

It helps to decide which of your goals are for the short term and which are for the long term. Short-term goals are things you need or want to buy soon, in the next few weeks. Your essential needs, such as bus rides or school lunches, are short-term goals. That is money you know you need to have available to spend. Another kind of short-term goal could be to have enough each week for a new book or the trading cards you love. You can have short-term savings goals, too. Maybe you want to save for a movie or a new baseball cap.

Other money goals will be stretched out over a longer time period, where you save money for several weeks, months, or years. These can be for purchasing bigger items, such as a new bicycle, a tablet, or a guitar. Some people even start saving for college or their first car years before they need them. Even though you are saving up for a long time, when you finally reach these goals and are able to buy what you dreamed of, it feels fantastic.

Vacations are expensive, so we need to save for them over a long period of time.

LITTLE STEPS

If you save just $5 a month, in two years, you will have saved $120.

NEED IT OR WANT IT?

Every time we go shopping, we make decisions. We decide which **brand**, color, or style of clothing we prefer. We decide if we can afford something. Sometimes, it can be harder to decide whether we should buy an item at all!

QUICK THRILLS

It can give us a thrill to buy something new. It is exciting to take it home and try it out. But have you ever been disappointed? **Have you ever found a video game a little boring after the first time you played it, or did a magazine keep you interested** for just half an hour? You may wonder if it was really worth the money you spent on it. Once we have spent our money, we cannot get it back. We only need to be disappointed a few times to learn that it is a good idea to think twice before we buy.

Stores create window displays to make us go in and spend our money. Think twice before you buy!

It's easy to fill your closet with clothes you don't really need — or even want! Try to only buy clothes you need and love.

ENOUGH IS ENOUGH

It can be hard to figure out the difference between needing something and really, really wanting it. You need food to fuel your body, but you don't really need donuts. You need clothes to keep you warm, but you don't need the latest fashionable brand of T-shirt, even if your friends have them. If you can learn to tell the difference between needing and wanting, you will be on your way to money-managing success.

This does not mean we should only buy the things we need and never buy things we want, though. Life would be a little boring without variety and special treats. The important thing is to know the difference between what you need and what you want. That way, when you are setting your goals, you do not get carried away. It's disappointing to buy something and later realize you don't really want it after all.

MONEY MATH

You have $5 to spend and you are in a used bookstore. Comics are 4 for $2 and books are $2.50 each. How much is each comic? How many comics could you buy if you also buy 1 book?

SEE PAGE 29 FOR THE ANSWER!

MAKE A BUDGET

To meet your goals, you will need a budget. This plan of action sets out how you will spend and save your money. A budget is really handy because once you have made one, you will not have to keep thinking so hard about your money. You just need to stick to your decisions once you've made them.

EXPENSES AND INCOME

Set your budget for each week. This is similar to your spending journal, so a notebook with lined pages is perfect for this. The first thing to do is write down all your basic expenses, those things you need to spend money on. This does not include things like treats. Make a "Fixed Expenses" column, and list what they are and the amounts. Add them up. Now do the same for your income, or money coming in. Write an "Income" heading, and list all the money that you know you will have, such as an allowance or paper route money. Write in the amounts, and add them up. How much money will you have left after your expenses? Subtract the "Expenses" total from the "Income" total. This is the amount you have to spend or save each week. Some people like to make savings part of their fixed expenses. This means they are sure to put that money away and will not be tempted to spend it. It is up to you whether you think you can afford to do it this way. If you do not have much left over each week, you might prefer to save a different amount each week. Getting into the habit of saving is the important thing.

SPENDING PLAN

With the money left, you can plan your spending. Make another heading for "Other Expenses," and list all the things you would like to spend money on, such as books, clothes, or games. Write in the amounts, and add them up. Make sure you are not planning to spend more than you have. At the end of the week, go back to your budget. See if all your figures worked out.

Having a budget should stop you from spending more money than you have.

BIG BUDGETS

Governments make budgets, too. Their budgets are on a massive scale, dealing with billions of dollars, but the idea is just the same. They see how much money they have coming in from taxpayers and decide what they can afford to spend on services, such as highways, health care, and education.

GET REAL!

When we start to make a budget, we are full of good intentions. We probably plan to spend as little as possible, and save, save, save. It may look great on paper, but life is not always like that. When you make your budget, be realistic, and do not be too hard on yourself.

IMPOSSIBLE TARGET

Say you have $10 coming in each week, and your fixed expenses come to $3. That leaves you $7 to spend or save as you wish. If you budget to save $5 each week, you will be left with just $2 to spend. There isn't much you can buy with that. Some weeks, you may only spend $2, or even nothing at all. But planning to spend only $2 every week is not very realistic. The problem with setting an unrealistic budget is that you will quickly get fed up with the whole idea. It is much better to set a realistic target. It's fine to spend money on the small things you want sometimes. That's what your allowance is for!

You will find that you can enjoy saving just as much as spending.

SURPRISES

However well we plan for the future, we cannot always be in control. Sometimes life throws surprises at us—things we just could not have expected or planned for. They might be pleasant surprises, like finding $10 down the back of the sofa, or they might be unpleasant surprises. Adults often have to spend money in emergencies, such as when the washing machine breaks down or the car needs repairs.

You probably won't have many spending emergencies, but you might have some surprise expenses. Maybe your school decides to take a field trip and you decide you want to buy a souvenir or snack. When you set your budget, you should plan for some surprise expenses. You don't have to plan for large amounts of money, but it's good to keep a little set aside.

MONEY MATH

After you make a budget, you find you have $10 to spend for fun this week. If you plan on spending $1.50 on a comic book and $2.50 on a bottle of nail polish, how much do you have left for unplanned shopping this week?

SEE PAGE 29 FOR THE ANSWER!

19

BORROWING AND DEBT

Sometimes in life we need to borrow money. Have you ever needed to borrow a few dollars from your mom or dad to pay for something? Money we borrow is called a **loan**. We eventually need to pay the loan back. The amount we owe is called a **debt**. It is important to pay off debts as soon as we can.

NOT FREE MONEY

Businesses or banks that lend money to people charge them for borrowing. This extra amount is **interest**, which is a percentage of the amount you borrow. If you borrow $100, and the interest rate charged is 10% of the total, you will be charged $10 interest. That means you owe a debt of $110.

Adults borrow money in different ways. The biggest loan they usually take out is to buy a home. This kind of loan is made by a bank and is called a **mortgage**. The borrower pays it off over a period of many years, and when it is all paid off, they own their house or condominium. People who have a mortgage must pay a certain amount they owe each month. It must be at the top of the list of payments in their budget. If they fail to make their mortgage payments, they could eventually lose their home.

Another way people borrow money is on a **credit card**. This is a plastic card from the bank that you use in stores to spend money you do not have at the time.

Keep a record of loans people give you, and pay them back quickly.

Credit cards can be useful, but it is easy to go into debt if you aren't careful with them.

Every month, the bank tells you how much you have spent on your credit card. You should pay off the full amount if you can. If you do not, they charge you interest on the total. It is a very expensive way to borrow money. If you have several different debts, you should pay off the one that costs you the most first. That is the one that charges the most interest.

BUDGET FOR IT

Even if you have borrowed only a small amount of money from your family, when you budget, you need to include paying off your debts in your spending plan. People really appreciate it when you pay them back quickly, because it shows you are responsible about money and about your debts. It will help you develop good habits for life.

SCARY DEBT!

Many US households have a lot of debt. In 2016, households with credit card debt owed an average of more than $15,000.

KEEP IT FRESH

Now that you have a budget, you are in control. You will be amazed at how much easier it is to manage your money. Remember, though, that nothing stays the same for very long. As your money situation changes, you need to look again at your goals and your budget.

CHANGING TASTES AND NEEDS

Remember how you used to like playing with a toy that today you find boring? A few years ago, you probably liked different clothes, foods, and TV shows, too. That is because life is always changing. As we grow up, our tastes change. It's no different with our finances. We always need to have money, but we want to spend it on different things. Last year, you may not have thought much about saving your money. What was important to you was having enough to cover your basic expenses and a few treats. Your situation may have changed. Maybe a friend has asked you to join them on vacation this summer, and you want to save up some money for the trip.

REVIEW AND REVISE

Smart savers and spenders review their goals and budgets regularly. Take a look at all the elements in your budget. Has your income changed? As you get older, there are more chances to earn a few dollars helping others. You may also receive money as gifts for big achievements as you get older, such as graduating school. You will have more to spend, which means you will have more choices.

It is just the same as with your first budget. As you get older, you will probably have more basic expenses. For example, when you get your first job, you will have more income—but you may also need to pay for transportation to and from work.

Over time, you should revisit your spending and saving goals. As your income increases, it's a good idea to save more each week, too. It can make a big difference to the total we save over a long period of time, and we may not even notice the few dollars less we have to spend each week.

Our tastes change as we grow up. It is good to declutter and get rid of things you no longer want. You can donate many things you no longer need!

MONEY MATH

Last year, you had an income of $50 in January. It is your birthday month, so in addition to your $20 allowance, you received $30 as gifts. This January, your income is $70. You received $40 as birthday gifts, so how much is your allowance now?

SEE PAGE 29 FOR THE ANSWER!

GIVE TO CHARITY

We all know that it is good to share. If you have snacks and your friends are hungry, you know that it's kind to share your food. It helps your friends and that makes you feel good. You can share money, too!

LEARN TO GIVE

There are always people in the world who are less fortunate than us, who have fewer things or less money to live on. You may think that you have nothing to share, but you will be surprised. You can get in the habit of giving to others in many ways. These habits will stay with you as you grow up, so you can become a caring, giving adult.

REWARDS FOR ALL

You now know how to set your money goals and create a budget. It is a great idea to add giving to that budget, too. Even a little money can do a lot of good. You could put aside a jar labeled "**Charity**," and drop in some loose change each week. You will be surprised at how quickly the amount adds up. When the jar is full, count the coins. Now you can choose a cause to donate your money to. Research causes that you would like to support. Ask your friends, parents, and teachers. You might want to donate to a local project, so you can see for yourself the good it is doing in your neighborhood. You might want to give to a large charity that works with people in need in foreign countries or animals in danger. Whatever you choose, you will learn a lot about how other people live, and you will feel good about doing something to help the world.

Giving does not always have to be in the form of money. You can donate items you no longer use—such as clothes, books, and toys—to a charity thrift shop. The organization may give the items to children in need or sell them to make money for other work. Next time you have extra money in your budget, consider helping others in need.

SPREADING THE GOOD

Did you know that giving is contagious? Research shows that when people see others giving to charity or doing good, they are more likely to do the same themselves. That is another great reason to get into the giving habit.

Research charities that interest you. This one takes care of baby elephants in Africa who have lost their parents.

DO GOOD

It feels good to learn new money skills that put us in control of our cash. It can also feel good to wisely spend your money on something new, especially if you have wanted and saved up for it for months. Still, the excitement from spending can wear off after a while. If you already have two pairs of sneakers, getting a third pair is not that exciting. Helping others can be exciting, too, and that good feeling doesn't wear off.

SPREAD A LITTLE HAPPINESS

There are many ways you can spend your money to spread a little happiness. As we have seen, you can donate to charity. It's good to help those who are less fortunate than us, and you can really make a difference.

There is also a saying that "Charity begins at home." It means that we do not have to look very far to make a difference. Why not make the people you love happy by helping them out? You do not have to spend much. A little gift for your mom when she has been working hard will show her how much you care. It is the thought that will make her happy, not the size of your gift. You can treat your friend to a milkshake or something fun, especially when they are feeling down. Showing you care always feels good.

If you are generous with your friends, they will be generous with you.

A GREAT EXPERIENCE

Sometimes it is good to spend our money on experiences instead of on things. Going out can be expensive, so you could offer to contribute to the cost. You could take a friend to the movies, or you could organize a scavenger hunt for a group of friends. Write the clues, and hide the objects. You will have fun, and so will your friends.

Another way to support a friend is to sponsor them in a project they are doing. If a friend is doing a charity event, such as swimming laps in a race, you could sponsor them for each lap they finish. It will encourage your friend to achieve their goal. Being generous is a win-win thing — the person receiving the gift is happy because you have shown you care. You're happy, too, because giving to others feels great!

Spending money on shared experiences can give us memories that last forever.

MONEY MATH

There is a new movie out that you and your best friend really want to see together. Tickets cost $6. Your friend has only $4, so you offer to pay for the rest of her ticket. How much do you pay altogether, including the price of your own ticket?

SEE PAGE 29 FOR THE ANSWER!

BE MONEY SMART

Spending time thinking about money matters will help keep you in control. Knowing what, why, and when you are spending will help you throughout your whole life.

ALL SET

You have learned to think about your spending and saving, and to set yourself goals. Now you are ready to think twice about whether you really need something or just really want it. You can see that saving for the future can be just as rewarding as spending your money now. To reach your goals, you know how to make a budget and how to keep checking it as your money situation changes.

Giving and sharing should be a part of your money planning. There are charities for just about every aspect of life, from helping people with diseases or researchers looking for cures, to providing shelter for people experiencing homelessness or protecting animals that are in danger of dying out. Whatever cause makes you feel excited, there is a charity that you can support.

THE BEST THINGS ARE FREE

Money is important for all of us. We need enough of it to run our lives and to help us move forward. But even though money can help us do great things in the world, it is not everything. The happiest people in the world are not always the wealthiest. They are the people who value things that money cannot buy. There is nothing quite like spending a great time with the people we love — our family and friends. A beautiful view, a funny story, a walk in the woods — all these wonderful things are free. We need to spend our time wisely, in just the same way as our money.

Having fun with friends costs nothing but makes us happy. Most of the best things in life are free!

MONEY MATH ANSWERS

Page 7: It will take 6 weeks to save up for the skateboard.
Page 11: You received $310 in 12 months.
Page 15: Each comic costs 50 cents. You can buy 5 comics and 1 book.
Page 19: You have $6 for unplanned spending.
Page 23: Your allowance is $30 a month now.
Page 27: You pay $8.

GLOSSARY

afford To have enough money to pay for something.

basic Something that is necessary or very important.

brand A specific company's product.

budget A plan of how to spend money.

charity An organization that helps people in need.

credit card A plastic card from a bank that allows customers to borrow money to pay for things.

debt Owing money to someone else.

employer Someone you work for.

expenses Money we spend.

finances The money you earn, spend, and save.

income Money that is earned from work, investments, and business.

interest Money paid regularly by people who borrow money, to those that lend it to them.

loan Money that we borrow from a bank or a person.

mortgage A loan of money from a bank used to buy a house, condominium, or other property.

saving To put money aside in a secure place for the future.

FURTHER READING

BOOKS

Eagen, Rachel. *What Do I Want? What Do I Need?* St. Catherines, ON: Crabtree Publishing, 2016.

Furgang, Kathy. *National Geographic Kids Everything Money.* Washington, D.C.: National Geographic, 2013.

Hall, Alvin. *Show Me the Money: Big Questions About Finance.* New York, NY: DK Children's Books, 2016.

McWhorter Sember, Brette. *The Everything Kids' Money Book: Earn it, save it, and watch it grow!* Avon, MA: Adams Media, 2008.

WEBSITES

Due to the changing nature of Internet links, PowerKids Press has developed an online list of websites related to the subject of this book. This site is updated regularly. Please use this link to access the list:

www.powerkidslinks.com/msfk/goals

INDEX